BOA
EDITIONS LTD

THE MOON MAKES ITS OWN PLEA

# THE MOON MAKES ITS OWN PLEA

*Poems by*

WENDY MNOOKIN

AMERICAN POETS CONTINUUM SERIES, NO. 113

BOA EDITIONS, LTD. ☼ ROCHESTER, NY ☼ 2008

First Edition
08 09 10 11 7 6 5 4 3 2 1

For information about permission to reuse any material from this book please contact The Permissions Company at www.permissionscompany.com or e-mail perm-dude@eclipse.net.

Publications by BOA Editions, Ltd.—a not-for-profit corporation under section 501 (c) (3) of the United States Internal Revenue Code—are made possible with funds from a variety of sources, including public funds from the New York State Council for the Arts, a state agency; the Literature Program of the National Endowment for the Arts; the County of Monroe, NY; the Lannan Foundation for support of the Lannan Translations Selection Series; the Sonia Raiziss Giop Charitable Foundation; the Mary S. Mulligan Charitable Trust; the Rochester Area Community Foundation; the Arts & Cultural Council for Greater Rochester; the Steeple-Jack Fund; the Ames-Amzalak Memorial Trust in memory of Henry Ames, Semon Amzalak and Dan Amzalak; the TCA Foundation; and contributions from many individuals nationwide.

See Colophon on page 96 for special individual acknowledgments.

Cover Design: Daphne Poulin-Stofer
Cover Art: "The View" by Christina Parrett Brinkman
Interior Design and Composition: Richard Foerster
Manufacturing: Thomson-Shore
BOA Logo: Mirko

Library of Congress Cataloging-in-Publication Data

Mnookin, Wendy, 1946–
  The moon makes its own plea : poems / by Wendy Mnookin. — 1st ed.
      p. cm. — (American poets continuum series ; no. 113)
  ISBN 978-1-934414-14-9 (pbk.)
  I. Title.

PS3563.N66M66 2008
811'.54—dc22

2008017889

BOA Editions, Ltd.
Nora A. Jones, Executive Director/Publisher
Thom Ward, Editor/Production
Peter Conners, Editor/Marketing
Glenn William, BOA Board Chair
A. Poulin, Jr., Founder (1938–1996)
250 North Goodman Street, Suite 306
Rochester, NY 14607
www.boaeditions.org

# Contents

FOR JIMMY

# A Short Fable of the Year Before Last

All those different conversations,
and white lilacs, that first
summer riot. Then watermelon.
No one would listen.
Confusion grew.
Children wandered off
into complicated games
with ropes and knots.
This or that husband found his way
to someone new. Likewise the wives.
Day crumbled into its own kind of ruin.
I tried to get everything settled.
*Should*, the first-born, fought
in all its clamorous splendor
for top billing, but eventually had to admit
others grow up, too. Somewhere
a well-digger found water.
Bread in the ovens gave off fragrant peace.
Abashed, *should* assumed its place
in the list of what could
be accomplished, what couldn't.

# Morning, with Cat

Dawn. A few clouds, nothing
too overt. Day moves in
not slowly, but certainly

not fast. As morning
gathers density, trees assume
an outline of existence,

crenelated, many-hued.
This is the hour of possibility,
when it seems there might be time

to fathom each blade of grass,
sawtoothed, blunted,
each green and feathery fern.

Everything is innocuous,
charged. Shadows
cling to the backs of things.

I hold myself still,
hollow a space for sorrow,
while the cat flicks her tail

at birds who beat us to language.
At the shameless ferns, taking
a thousand years to tell their story.

# My Day

My back against the droning
of the fridge, I sit on the kitchen floor
and survey my day. Coffee brews,
steady in the pot. Dust under the sink
claims the curls of its own life.

Outside, a cement truck churns,
bees swarm the apple tree.
They ignore petals washed down
by last night's rain, lying
on the path in seductive scatter.

Or I think they do. It may be safe
to go barefoot, it may not.
The cement truck rustles and shifts
its opinion. Bees dispute
in the heat of their beauty.

## Was It Ever As Good As It Was?

I used to believe earth rocks like a cradle,
pouring in the tides, rolling them back out.

And why not? If I filled a bowl with water
and tipped it first one way, then the other,

I could create tides, sweep myself away,
my inner magnet tilted, worldstruck.

I can still get lost a mile from home,
every streetlight yellow, every marquee dark.

I try to keep myself
from taking a familiar turnoff, the usual

excuses of the past. So what if the sun
drowns in the horizon, disappearing with a sound

like someone trying not to make any sound at all.

# Reef

We have wetsuits.
We have our marriage in front of us,
glittering. All the same,

I keep an eye on the boat,
watch for water to rise,
or fall. And what about sharks,

those hammerheads, *harmless*,
you tell me. Your voice carries
on a turquoise wave. I'd like to be brave,

but it seems like a big decision
to make out here in the middle of nowhere.
Underwater, with its promises,

its erratic light, your face
looks strange—closer than it really is,
or farther away, I can't tell.

Only that the distance between us
is not what I imagined.
Escape is already populated

by bubbles of air you exhale
mixing with bubbles I exhale,
the churn of water as you move

sloshing into the churn as I move.
Water changes to accommodate us
and we are equally complicit in the change,

equally engulfed. Even my hand,
held before my face, looks moody, detached.
What are we coming into?

What are we leaving?
On the bright linear beach
marshes smell like failure.

## Partial Praise for Tropics

Sunning on flat rocks, Galapagos
Sea Lions bark out summons

or warning. Seaweed
entices my calves, while buried in sand

ridged shells whorl their patterns
like Braille, stunning

my fingertips. Everywhere
something offers itself. Who knows,

who ever really knows,
what causes a person

to shy away? The Flightless
Cormorant spreads its stubby wings

to dry them. Poor baby—
but why *poor baby*? A bird

doesn't know to feel different.
Does it?

I love the world, its intricacies and maneuvers—

how could I *not* praise a God
who assigned the Frigate Bird

an inflatable scarlet sac beneath its beak?—
but I need removal,

a reticent God
who leaves almost everything unsaid.

Not this carnival of color, sharp
and precise, every

wingtip and beak competing.
Even one eye closed doesn't do it.

## Anything Warm

Anything warm is warm.
Anything red has something to say.
Anything that drifts also smudges,
like secrets. That intense.
Anything loose is a message,
endless, and endlessly enticing.
Anything narrow gets there first.
Especially anger. Anything watery
pleads, though the story stays
buried under its layers, obscuring
whatever it is we've done
to deserve this. In the eternal life
of regret, Sunday looks back.
Monday is certainty,
with a mystery inside out.
Anything two days in a row
sings the same song I do
without repeating the first verse.
Because there is no return.
That seems dramatic, but likely.
Just look at the waves,
all moving in one direction.
It made Noah crazy!
Another day—hell, another
hour—he'd be ready
to wring that dove's neck.
What right did she have
to exhaustion, to twittery musings?
One declarative sentence
would be a relief.

## Second Thoughts

*Let's go to Plum Island,*
you say. Well, maybe
for the thrill of finding red
on the chest of a Wood Warbler.

The sky cooperates
and clears itself of threat.
The ride home complicates.

Once I nursed a newborn squirrel
the cat brought in from the woods.
It was a present,
and I tried to see it that way.
I fed it with an eyedropper,
sheltered it in an old sock,
named it Fred,
Fred Gray,
and watched it die.

Who ever knows what to do?
All this time I could have been
planting, careful
to feel for the wisp of roots,
settle the bulbs in the ground
right-side up.

# Rental

The children spend hours
peeling sunburnt skin from each other's backs.
I lie on the deck, astounded
by red, roses draping over the trellis,
heavy as fruit.

Sand castles grow more elaborate—
winding moats, turrets.
*Come in, come in, it's time for dinner,*
my voice lost in the greed of ocean air.

You walk along the beach,
down where waves harden the sand
and make it easier to grip.
At night I dream you keep walking

until you disappear beyond the last piling.
The dream tells me you're dead
so I can't be angry.

I wake up angry.
Where is the light switch?
Where is a cup for water?

Over the couch, a shawl romanticizes peacocks.
Three flat rocks wait it out in a soap dish.

## Biking Through Haze

I stare at my feet, watching
the road under me for sand.
When I look up, you're gone.

When I was a child,
death was my bed
losing the weight of me.
My chair. My hairbrush
with nothing to do.
Such a lonely feeling,
molecules missing
their center, me.

The sun is who she is,
solid, hot.
A deer in the woods
stares long at me
before she bolts.
It's the summer of gypsy moths,
trees restless. Everywhere
cocoons tighten their grip.

It was you who said,
*Let's go on a bike ride.*
Or did you say, *I'm going.*

# Coyotes

It gets dark earlier each day
so really, it would be better
if you could come back. Come back
before I need a flashlight to walk the dog.

Come back before the outlines of table and chair
recede into background,
before all that's left
to remind me who I am
is the smell of winter through a broken pane.

There are coyotes on the golf course.
They know what they want, completely
and freely who they are, unconcerned
with my steady trudge.

You'd better come back.
How lonely would I be
without the danger
of you. The clink of ice in your bourbon.
Your hand, not quite absent-
mindedly, on mine.

## Small Failure

And even then, it might be
too heavy to carry.
It might need a wagon,
a red one, you know the kind.
It might need a truck.

It might lie in a box,
the box might be wrapped,
it might be tied with a bow.
As if that changes anything.

Could it be too small?

What about berries—
if there's a way to keep birds from those bushes,
it doesn't look like I'll live long enough to learn it.

The fields wait for ruin.
The birds don't wait.
In a corridor of blue light,
they strip the bushes of all the berries

while bees rise from their nest
like origami, glittery
and intricate with intention.
My intention has always been to love,
even with my hand swollen
and packed in mud.

## Ongoing

You want me to agree
to an open window when we sleep,
even on the coldest nights.
I want you to bring me water,
but not care if I drink it.

You want me to love,
as much as you do,
the sapling you planted.
Someday, from our bed, we'll see
blossoms, then fruit.

But tonight
there's no hot water in the shower.
It's heart-stopping
cold, and me, in it.
Isn't that something
you should be able to fix?
When I manage a full breath

I have to admit
it's bracing, and somehow ennobling,
as if I diverted the hot water on purpose
so I can emerge pinker than a newborn, ready
to love someone again, maybe myself.

Wrapped in a towel
I inch open the window—
I can afford to be generous—
then drop the towel
and dive into bed.

Come on, help me out here.
Thanks for the glass of water,
but I'm shivering in the sheets

and the apple tree's spindly,
bark on the trunk peeling away in strips.

# Sailing at Summer Camp

I knew the difference between coming
about and jibbing, but I forgot
the boy's name, was too shy to ask.
His bare back peeled in papery drifts.
My head pounded from staring
into the sun, from sweat
and sun cream and silence
as we sat on either side of the tiller.
I bent to tie my sneaker—
it was cooler at the bottom of the boat—
and saw a penis
dangling through the loose leg
of his swim trunks.
I undid my laces, looked again
while it played its usual games,
a little orbit, some torque.
The sails luffed. It took a long time
to get back to who I was.

## Bringing the Flowers Inside

Lilies
require a glass vase
to see through.

They do
what they like. They breathe,
they open,

they spill
their pollen and their scent.
I avoid

the hallway,
where lilies squander themselves.
Bunched in blue-

patterned pitcher,
zinnias are hectic with display.
Even when they fade,

they fade earnestly—
red and orange, gold.
As they were

all along.
As they are. So pure and honest,
thistles refuse

gaudy refinements,
stake a claim in the rocky corner.
They know

what they're doing
and do it hard. They have lived
long enough

to earn this.
Clematis twine their tendrils
in a long

ribbon of sleep.
Oh what kind of person
am I, striding

with such purpose
from the garden, clutching clematis
in my hand?

It was wanting
that made me. Wanting that
started this, anyway.

# French Café

The night was hardly cooled
by the sun's going down.
I took off my sandals
and slung them, dangling
from one finger, over my shoulder.

You called me *Sexy* then.
I could feel my name
in the heat from the sidewalk
that burned my feet.
You couldn't pay me
to put those shoes back on.

Stars dripped onto the roof
of your fourth-floor walk-up,
somewhere trees
enacted the jazzy jigsaw
of branch and sky.

Barefoot, whispering,
we climbed back down
to the French café on the first floor,
kitchen always left unlocked,
and inched open
the heavy refrigerator door.

From those thick creamy plates—
the scent of sugar in your hair—
we stole a Linzer torte,
a slice of chocolate cake.

Not *Sweetheart*. Not *Honey*.
Not even *Love*.

# August

A house finch darts
from hollyhock to hollyhock.
bending each tall stem.
Flowers scatter themselves
without even trying—
there are lilies under the apple tree,
lamb's ears by the porch.
Butterflies ignore the butterfly bush
and fend for themselves. Mint
grows wild. A hummingbird
swoops, captivated
by my bright red shirt.
Take off your clothes.

# At Sea

At the end of the jetty.

Where the boats come in. Where the boats go out. At the pile of rocks that swallows the sun at the end of the day.

At the turn of the trail. At the last dune.

In front of the hot-dog stand. At the door to the pub. By the shanty, the shipbuilder's yard, the discarded yellow boots, the smashed
clam shells.

You thought I'd give in to despair.
But today is today, everywhere I look. And I look everywhere.

## The Way Back

The dog loves me, but not as much
as she loves earth's deep smell,
drawn to the surface in leafy sediment.
She whines and paces in the back of the car.

I keep driving.
The left front tire is exhausted.
The fender worries for its own shiny skin.
My window is raised into privacy.
Upholstery pleads.

The dog's still whining.
I was two when my father died,
thrown from the car. There is nothing
I can promise her that she understands.

The tire could give out completely.
A geometry of mood rolls like a stone
down the hill, gathering speed.
The mirror resists an urge to avert its eyes.

# Skating

At the pond, my dead stare
through thick, dirty ice,
wet hair slapping

their frozen cheeks.
It's taken a long time
for them to find me.

They have no intention
of leaving. I cannot
attend to the choreography

of their need—
my fingers are numb,
my breath catches. Tired

of waiting, they break
through ridged ice,
fling themselves

into the drama of figure-eights.
Even more blatant
than they were in life,

they clutch in their woven fingers
everything I've done
without them—

the dream of mountains,
late afternoon.
I have given sorrow

a lifetime and a day
to shrink into its valved pocket,
and still my superstitious

childhood rests in me
like water. The dead spin,
faster, faster.

# Spill

Milk drips from the table.
I do not reach
for a cloth, do not

bend to clean it up.
I place my bowl in the sink
gently, as if it were alive.

My father died
because of something
I was. Being a child

was no excuse.
There's no denying
I wore my pink

pop-it beads,
fell asleep
sucking my thumb.

The child never forge
never forgives.
She can be silent

for longer than I can.
Even now, my best chance
of hearing her

is at night, in the rustling
of trees
trading their needled secrets.

Who can sleep?
A ladybug crawls along a wall
hoping for luck.

The child shrugs,
*your house is on fire,*
*your children alone.*

# Makeshift

I.

My parents' refrigerator holds
orange juice and 2% cottage cheese.
A box of raisins. Batteries.
*Let's go shopping,* I say.

It's raining.
Mother can't find her umbrella
or her car keys.
We drive my car
past the garden, past peonies
laying their bruised heads along the ground.

At the store we buy eggs and milk,
sliced turkey, bread.
We buy Granny Smith apples and bananas.
*Who will eat all this?* Mother asks.

2.

Mother wants me to take the coffee table
sitting, unused, in the basement.
I've always loved its curved wooden legs,
that secret drawer.

She's content—she promises me—
with the brass table she took
from her mother's house.

I lash the table to the top of the car,
pull the ropes tight.


3.


At home, the sky threatens, and threatens,
but doesn't release. The teapot's whistle
accosts a few hardy birds,
who rise in tumult.
The dog turns over her bowl,
my heart unravels one more wish.

It is what it is.
Even the sparrows have found a way.
In a windblown puddle,
they dip, and dip again,
bending and ruffling in the makeshift lake.

# Thanksgiving

*One glass of wine is good for you,*
Mother says. And three are too many.
No one needs to leave the table
crying. Salt takes out the stain.
Or is it sugar?

The cat meows,
plaintively, repetitively.
Come in. Go out. Outside

the boundaries are clear.
I listen hard to the hiss
of the sun's longing,
red leaves etched
by that other brilliance, sky.

## Maybe I Made This Up

My mother said, *Yes, you can*
*wheel your baby sister*

*that far, and back.*
The baby blew fish kisses

with her small round mouth
while I pumped high on the swings,

and higher. *Hello!* I waved
when I hung by my knees

on the jungle gym.
*Yippee-yeah!* I called

when I herded the cattle
downstream,

over the seesaw, around the sandbox,
past the distant fountain.

At home my mother asked
*Where's your sister?*

and the world shifted
slightly. If

there were clouds,
they fled. If birds,

they silenced.
I can only tell you

the truth as I know it.
Last week an ice cream store

opened in my town,
and I wrote to my kids

about another opening,
years ago, when they were allowed

to walk four blocks
for free ice cream,

and each of them wrote back,
one at a time,

no, I was twelve,
I was seven,

it was summer, or vanilla,
or strawberry.

I raced with my mother
to the park and found

my sister, batting
her toys in the carriage.

Just before my mother
grabbed her, my sister

looked at me, she
saw who I was, she

didn't look away.

# My Sister, My Childhood Ally

Choking on a hard candy
when she was two, my sister,
my childhood ally, turned blue
and waved her hands frantically,
trying to funnel in air. My stepfather

grabbed her by her ankles
with one huge hand, so she jerked
off the floor and hung there, trembling
over her fate. He raised his other hand
and whacked her between her shoulders

while she twisted in his grip. He
whacked again and my mother
came running, pulling her robe
around her bare breasts, *What happened?*
*What happened?* Beyond them,

where I looked through the window,
the brave girls at Brearley School
lined up to wait for the bell,
though the clang never failed
to startle, and the heavy door stuttered

as it opened. Was the world ever safe?
When was that? In their blue jumpers
and starched white shirts,
those girls looked competent
and grown-up, ready to take

what the day, in its random hurry,
offered. Not one of them ran.
I shifted from foot to foot
waiting to see if luck would love
my sister, if it would marry her

as she vomited onto the floor, and breathed.

# Manhattan, 1952

Because she was born
somewhere in Russia,
and walked across mountains
and changed her name, Great
Aunt Dora serves tea, not coffee,
in cups that are flowered,
and chipped. When I ask
if she has crayons to draw with,
she says, *I don't, my darling,*
and gives me three blue envelopes
so I can have the stamps
for my collection. Great Uncle
Herman is a dentist. They have lots
of paintings on the walls, because
people pay him with paintings,
not money. Mother thinks
money would be better.
I like the painting of him
with his hat on, even though
he's indoors. When it's time
to go, Great Aunt Dora
kisses my forehead with a smell
like peaches. At home I sit
by the Christmas tree, because
Christmas is for everyone,
and peel stamps from Germany
and Poland, fasten them in my stamp
collector's book. I am a small
thing in the drama. Born at the end
of the Second World War, I am named
for Wendy Darling, in *Peter Pan,*

who ran away to Neverland
by thinking only lovely,
wonderful thoughts.

# Other People I Could Have Been

A lighthouse keeper, my dreams crusted with salt.

A drawbridge operator, strict attentiveness
punctuated by stretches of inner life.

A farmer, raising goats, making cheese
I sell from a roadside stand
under a sign that says, *Cheese.*

A meter maid, one day forgiving,
retributive the next.

A country music singer with a gravelly voice
and a lost guitar.
It stays lost for years.

A sailor. A junkie. A maker of collage.

Intention is all—
imagine the path of a bullet to its target, the world
narrowing to nothing but *zing.*
It doesn't feel like sin.
Completion maybe. Or promise.

I'm getting hungry, and thirsty.
Bored. Or what I often mean
by bored—scared.
What can my life still encompass?
There's a slow ache
in the muscles of my back
and in the coiled muscle of my heart.

The cat knows my ways.
Humming with the temperature
of her own being, she settles onto my lap,
almost an oracle, not too obscure.
Giving good news. My allotted share.
Never more than that.

# First Marriage

I drank water loaded with ice,
pressing the glass to my forehead
against the Arizona heat.
Our neighbors to the left
drank martinis. Our neighbors
to the right drank milkshakes, but only
on payday. When I got a fever
and chills, and couldn't keep anything
down, my husband—on his way
to med school—said it was not
unexpected. *Different bacteria
in Arizona water,* he said.
He said, *You'll get used to it.*

They said it didn't matter,
how hot it got in Tucson. Everything
was air-conditioned. At dusk, the hills
behind married-student housing
changed from scruffy brown to purple.
I hiked up there, the switchback
all rocks and gravel, searching
for a shift in the air. Halfway
around the world, Marines dug in
at Khe Sanh for no reason anyone
knew. The hills that hemmed them in,
taken, lost, lost again,
used to be canopied with white,
with every shade of green.

# Pregnant Woman on the Beach

I can't see what she's holding
in her hands, whether the children,
gathered around her, hover in excitement

or fear. She's humming.
How bad could it be? Please, not
a fish, mangled, the bleeding mouth,

that desperate eye. I move closer
and see a spider, ragged, map itself
across her palms. I hate spiders—

crusty shell, hairy legs.
How to tell the poisonous
from the plain? My heart,

which had been thrumming along
in dark privacy, revels in attention,
more than I can give. If I could be

her hands, that steady, her hair,
self-contained in a coil around her head,
but the future backs away, leaving me

jittery, hurried. The children lose
interest in the spider, run ahead.
I call my children *children*,

though they're grown.
I call them often, sometimes
forgetting why. There are dangers,

many I can't name. Sun
washes color from her eyes,
color I long for, or long to remember.

Clouds shift, exchanging likenesses.

## And This Is Just the Beginning

If there are going to be clouds
let's have them dark and skittery,
roiling across the sky
with no purpose but their own.

The wind doesn't give a damn.
It's all shift and spin
and gleeful self-pleasuring.

The ceiling fan?
One more tick as it circles
its ineffective life away
and that fan is history.
It's had its chance

and now it's my turn for a brouhaha,
a glass thrown across the room
while you stand masked with shaving cream,
almost a statue.

What did you do?
You're there, aren't you,
your very own blood
coursing through your very own body?
I'm going to stand in the middle of my life
and feel nothing
stitch its needs to mine.

When I slam the door behind me
my life becomes more spacious.
All day I carry this with me.

I do not open the door,
I do not sweep it up.

# The Shortest Day of the Year

Our doors blocked by a blizzard
the two of us climbed from a window
into a world made new—

mailboxes buried, signs disappeared.
We walked on the tops of bushes,
dug until we found our car.

And dug some more.
We cleared the hood,
unburdened the windshield,

tunneled all the way to the tires.
Then what?
The roads were closed,

there was nowhere to go.
Sweating inside our layers,
we let ourselves fall

back into drift.
We had no ambition.
For minutes, or a year,

it was enough to lie there,
stunned with sun, with implacable white.
Our eyes glazed.

The frost of our breath happened.
And then we stood, clapping
our jackets free of snow,

suddenly shy
to see the imprint of wings,
so slight, it's a wonder

we trusted ourselves at all.

## After Thirty Years

When we walk back from the field
at night, the dog pulling us along,
I see it for a second in your face—

you stare into our windows
as if you're a stranger
all over again, all over again
balancing the equation of who you are.

If it's easy, what's the point?
On Saturday we could walk in the woods
where it's so icy
even the dog can't keep from falling.

And then, for reward,
you can peel me an apple
the way you do,
unraveling the skin in one unbroken spiral.
Trick of removal, trick of provision.

You think we'd like it, a world
of sharp grace, immediate and realized?

## Part of a Longer List

Last winter the tomato seeds I planted
in trays under special lights
sprang up too quickly
and withered before spring.

I love tomatoes
on the vine, their smell of dirt and heat.

I love peas, snapped and eaten.
The insistence of sun.
I love clouds, their refusal
to stay put. And the staying
of a view through a single pane of glass.

I used to love drawers,
their many secrets.
The way tinfoil could be thinned
to a smooth shine
by rubbing with a fingernail.

I loved the speed of letters
dropped in the chute from the fifth floor.
The mystery of arrival,
and of shoelaces tied too fast.

The times table, especially nines,
one digit rising on the left,
while on the right,
without dismay, another fell.

I loved to play jacks,
the temperamental bounce of the ball,
sweeping the jacks into my hand.
I practiced in my sleep,
which, it turns out, wasn't enough.

# Something

There's something, there's always
something. A sunset, a meal,
the longest car ride in the history

of family vacations, some tag
that will perfectly fit
a certain time in our lives—

FIVE OF US IN ONE TENT WITH THE DOG—
the people I loved most
in one small space, smelling

of wet dog, and together.
Until the older boy unfolded himself
from his sleeping bag, slowly

unzipped the tent flap—
is there any way to zip quietly?—
and went outside, again, to pee.

Branches broke under his feet.
Silence. And then
the fitful hissing onto leaves

before he threaded his way back.
I want to remember
what I want to remember—

how I lay in the tent, listening,
until it seemed I could see
our breathing in the humid dark,

each separate strand
and entwined pattern.
But the world insists on being

what it is. Slipping from us,
my son untangled, again,
and left. Tall pines shadowed

a resemblance of themselves,
a skeletal suggestion,
upper boughs taken on faith

somewhere above him in the night.
I hated those trees, their assumptions,
what they said about afterwards.

# The River Scrapes Against Night

Through the scrim of the tent
I map constellations, fearful
I may have missed one
of the bland white sheep
lined up for counting,
fuzzy with their own bleating fatigue.
No matter how hard I stare,
I can't find the boundaries
between river and canyon,
canyon and sky. Bats
swoop close, intimate,
alarming. Night keeps knocking
without a hint of politeness.
I'm not fooled
by steady breathing.
We are this small.
This brief.

# Hammered Band with Tapered Edges

My friend's daughter has a toe ring
and she knows where I can get one
so we go upstairs to look on the internet
where I find I need to measure
with a cut-out paper strip
the size of my second toe below the knuckle
the two of us trying not to laugh
as we nudge the paper around my toe
but laughing anyway
in this house where everyone whispers
though none of us knows
what my friend wants
if she'd prefer silence or laughter
she's downstairs dying
can't blink *yes* or *no*
the nurse can't ask her
do you want to die now
the nurse can ask
but it's too late
we've waited too long
she can't tell.

# Hard-Backed Chair

We've been having the same fight
for decades. I don't believe it
anymore, not really,

but it may be the last
good fight
we have in us. So

when I'm tired,
and dark arrives before four,
and harlequin frogs

are dying out,
not from global warming
exactly, but from algae

that proliferate because of global
warming, when Liz has spent
her twentieth day

in the hospital, then
I have no patience
for your silences, no time.

Why can't you
share your feelings?
Liz is dying.

I turn my back to the window
and cry—there's so much
to mourn for—

while you go to Liz's hospital room
and sit in that chair
all night

and when she wakes,
terrified, you tell her
she isn't dead.

## From My Window

While my friend is dying
my neighbors are standing—

one with a new puppy,
one with a baby—

in a winter sun so sudden
it makes my eyes tear.

I can't hear them talking
but I watch their quick gestures,

the angling of their heads.
Happy, that's what they are, happy

to be just where they are, in the middle
of February, surrounded by snowmelt.

Even the puppy gets it—
especially the puppy—

and jumps up
and hooks his front legs over the stroller

making the baby chortle in silent-
movie delight. Not me. No chance

I'll be tangled in the puppy's leash,
tripping over *if,*

over *wouldn't it be nice*. Soon enough
stars will blink themselves dizzy,

and the melting snow, unaccustomed
to such flamboyant unfolding, will freeze

into black ice that glitters
only sometimes, and not when you fall.

## On Her Knees

Blue ignores warnings,
wants another chance.
There is none.
Blue must be taught.
Blue must be willing to compromise.

White has the patience of caves,
owl spoor, bones of the mouse
bleached almost colorless.
My friend grabs at that patience
and bites down, hard.

Brown doesn't have to prepare.
Brown has spent lifetimes
shifting sand into the sea,
taking the sand back.
Brown is ready

but red, that gulping heart
with only one lifetime,
wants more.
One more summer, one more fall.

In October, at the grave, yellow exceeds.

Green bends close, whispering promises.
I'll have none of it.

## First They're Mad

The dead come back fisted,
ready for a fight.

As if I'd done something.
As if whatever it is I did

I could undo. I plead
with a hint of reproach—

they are, after all, dead.
I don't know how much more

they can take. My four o'clock
sorrow, for instance.

My games of pretend.
Though I wouldn't have guessed it,

the dead soften their stance.
They shake out their hands,

flatten their palms together
into a prayer only they

understand. Who left whom
is a matter for another day.

In their world, there's a name for it,
which we could try to think of

here, with our sunsets still intact.
They have a world of sunsets,

eternity glowing on the horizon,
but they're used to it. It's the binding

they're still getting used to.
The weaving and binding, one soul

to another, dead and living,
living and dead. Those sunsets

can go on forever, and they do,
which provides a lift,

a little necessary distraction.
Or doesn't.

The dead support the world.
Doesn't that break your heart?

## Holding Something Back

A breeze comes through the curtains
the way I always hoped it would—

not insistently, but steadily,
changing the view. The girl I was

comes home, slender,
with long straight hair and barefoot,

trailing a scent of cut grass.
She kisses me on both cheeks.

The air shifts,
holding something back.

Birds abandon the branch.
I don't know what to do.

I'm the same person I was
but I'm missing myself.

The earth is, in her own way,
lonely. Or hungry.

Pray for rain,
or lie in the sun, soaking it up?

Stay or go?
Stay or stay.

In the space of that indecision,
lifetimes slip by.

# Flax

Laundry hangs out its stripes,
the counter shines. Even the cat
feels the satisfaction of Tuesday.

For his third birthday
my son asked for a white cake.
I baked angel food,
brought recipe and egg whites and beater
to the cabin in Maine.

He cried when he saw it.
He meant a not-chocolate cake.
He meant a yellow cake.

I heat the oven for bread,
measure flour and flax,
proof the yeast in warm milk.
Apples plead for their skin, thin

and necessary covering.
When I wash my hands,
flax seeds cling to my fingers,
the hems of my sleeves.

Gathered in deep waiting, seeds
have all the time in the world.

## Blue

There were buildings,
and rooms in those buildings,
and in the beginning
it seemed the rooms were perfect
to contain us.

And then you fell
and cracked a rib.
I said, *It doesn't hurt.*
I looked at your face and said,
*It doesn't hurt much.*
Blame adhered like a bandage,
calming me.

It was never just the two of us.
There's sky behind the buildings
and smoke and flames
and people who jump
from those buildings,
some of them holding hands.

Some days I try to live
knowing, really knowing,
the worst can happen.

I should have touched your rib
gently, the way I am going to imagine
God touched Adam's rib
to make a partner.

If I can imagine *God*.
If I can imagine *gently*.

# When Three Stars Can Be Seen in the Sky

Is it too much to hope
the cat will come out from under
the night with its alternate world
and lie on my lap, and recognize me?

Too much to hope my stepfather will eat
more than a few spoons of pudding?

To be sated with reason and routine.
To walk to the corner store,
purchase a quart of milk.

Clouds tumble and push into rushing.
Church bells are loud with slow industry.
Long after they quiet, they echo in my head.

Some things don't allow second chances.
In time, even the silent bells will be silent.

## Measured Spaces

Love was small inside me,
allowing only itself. The cat
was old, and pissed on everything—
down comforter, couch, living room rug.
I decided to put her down.

Did the cat dream herself
lazy on the lawn?
I dreamed a breeze through a window
ruffling white curtains.
When the vet came

time refused to move
at anything but its usual pace.
I held her close, pressed to my chest.
What she knew, and what I wanted
her to know, may have been different.

Surely were different.
She fell into the hole I dug,
though I tried to lower her gently.
I marked her grave with a rock,
imperfectly round.

## Done with It

The cat was old when she died,
her eyes rheumy,
the paunch of her stomach brushing the floor,
but after she'd been dead a few months
her eyes cleared.
She thinned.

Though she still loved sun,
she stopped sleeping away the day
in a nest of light by the window.
Her ears pricked at the slightest sound.

She began to chase the dog again
up and down the hallway,
around the table
and through all the arguments they'd ever had,
whisking under a chair
when she'd had enough.

I almost stopped missing her
when I missed again
her weight on my feet in bed at night,
her refusal to shift,
even when I tried to loosen her,

until there it was again,
need. Want
was a different four-letter, one-syllable word

and the pane was cold
where I leaned my forehead against the window

until, impatient
with the mess that longing makes,
I wiped my breath from the glass.

## A Pond of Peaches

You said *a pond of peaches*
and I took them
from your hands, I floated

in an indulgence of peaches.
It was June. There was time.
But you said

*a pound of peaches,* you said
I moved the plane tickets
from your desk. You're so sure

I moved those tickets,
I start to wonder
if I did, and what else

I may have done—
some slight, some lack
that gave you the tumor

while I stood around
like a desert, refusing you water,
even a mirage of water.

## Big Dipper

When the nurse allows you
three sips of water, you
raise your head toward me.
I say, into the stubble of your beard,
*Fine. Everything's fine.*

Last night I couldn't sleep.
I went into your study,
stood beside the window
with its untried view.
In the charity of cold,
sky reached
with some sort of promise.
Stars agreed
to consuming separateness.

What are the dimensions
of solitude? The sky so large
I pinned myself to the one
constellation I know,
its slow drip of solace—
the second star in the handle,
a single burn against black,
is really two.

# Not a Spider

Lot's wife,
what did the backward glance
get her? In that kind of heat,
any mistake can be costly.

Did the moon stay
a sliver? Who can tell
what happened, and why?

In the beginning
there were plans, in the
beginning there were formulations.
But the effort it took
to keep going! To remain
disappointed.

She thought she'd made a deal.
She was willing
to weave small intricate webs,
to reach between two blades of grass,
the edges of a windowpane.
It was enough.

A pillar of salt?
Who said anything
about a pillar of salt?
And to be clear:
she didn't give a damn
about the grateful birds,
or the many-colored lizards
lapping at her feet.

# The Moon Makes Its Own Plea

Nothing gets done
except existence. Sky
with its undirected patience.
Light carrying on
from window to window.

There are ashes in the fireplace.
I hold the grit of my life in my hands.
The starlings, chattering wildly,
witness, but cannot grant.

What chance do I have
against perfection? Even Jacob
would not let the Angel go
without a blessing.

Last night I woke myself from a dream
crying, *Let me stay!*

Ditto the moon.

# And So I Decide to Study Hebrew After All

Like favorite uncles, the letters.
consort without me. I sweep my eyes
from right to left, expecting welcome,
but they laugh at their own jokes,
sip their special tea
through cubes of sugar held
between their teeth. I move my lips,
lost, until *Lamed* waves me over,
cane raised high. I lean against him,
his woolen smell, stare at *Shin*
with the flaming hair. *Vav* is the skinny one.
*Gimel* is frayed at the cuffs. *Tzadi*,
who's been sneaking schnapps,
lists to one side. *Mem* props him up.
And *Kaf*. Breathing vowels, *Kaf*
places his palm on my head
and goes on talking.

# The Weatherman on TV

wishes Happy Birthday
to Lucy Miller in Abilene, Texas.
Here in Boston

clouds abandon
their flagrant show, the weather,
as always, changeable

and lonely. My grandmother
bragged, *I used to walk to school*
*four miles in rain or snow.*

She lived to be a hundred.
I thought my mother was old
when she was thirty-five,

a distant condition involving
matching hats and shoes,
so many appointments.

I can't brag
about walking through rain,
because there is

no rain here, just sprinklers
doing a steady imitation,
convincing enough

to spray a rainbow across the lawn.
It's time
to set the dogs to howling,

command clouds
into their own nature.
When I get through, believe me,

umbrellas will be a blessing.
I'll live to be a hundred
in some metaphysical Texas

walking miles
in a hat I'd never wear.
under a sun I've never known.

# Respite

I do not mean to boast
of bad times, or good.
Only that we are here,
in the absolute space of our bed,
our knees content
to leave the distance of a single cell
between us. The dog whimpers
as she chases something
in her sleep. When I call to her
she takes a hiccuping breath
and quiets. You shift
and fold yourself around me,
your arm pressing
the small of my back.
I leave it there.
I let the crick in my neck
remember small victories—
oceans, comfortable shoes.
Even the routes we organized,
leaving time for rest,
a little solitude.

## Tricks of Color and Light

Extremity, with all its vivid
demands, has eased. Moss
dreams of the swollen creak of the swing.
The swing dreams of the child
who loves that swing and now lies sleeping,
no longer a child. Soothed
by the weight of summer,
the branching willow
and the ground it stands in,
the walls and windows of our house,
where every eave and gutter
bleeds into sameness, chrysanthemum
dream in the language of burning.
On the bedside table, a pitcher of water
and a bowl of ripe figs
dream the slow scent of time,
aftertaste slipped from words.
I have been thinking again
that one of us will die first,
leaving the other alone.
Mice rummage in the attic.
Rain drips in the gutter, unaware.

# Acknowledgments

Thanks to the editors of the following publications where poems appeared, sometimes in earlier forms:

*Bellevue Literary Review*: "On Her Knees";
*The Big Ugly Review*: "Coyotes";
*Blood Lotus*: "Maybe I Made This Up," "Spill";
*The Comstock Review*: "Skating";
*Dark Sky Magazine*: "The Shortest Day of the Year";
*Del Sol Review*: "Something";
*The Florida Review*: "The Weatherman on TV";
*Full Circle Journal*: "Big Dipper";
*The Greensboro Review*: "Was It Ever As Good As It Was?";
*Harvard Review*: "The Moon Makes Its Own Plea," "My Sister, My Childhood Ally";
*Hurricane Alice*: "First Marriage";
*LocusPoint*: "A Pond of Peaches," "Blue," "Flax," "French Café," "Not a Spider";
*Moment*: "And So I Decide to Study Hebrew After All," "Manhattan, 1952";
*Poetry Motel*: "Sailing at Summer Camp";
*Pool*: "Anything Warm," "Biking Through Haze";
*Prairie Schooner*: "A Short Fable of the Year Before Last," "Pregnant Woman on the Beach," "Reef," "Thanksgiving";
*Rhino*: "Makeshift";
*Runes*: "The River Scrapes Against Night";
*Salamander*: "At Sea," "Hammered Band with Tapered Edges," "Measured Spaces";
*Soundings East*: "August";
*West Wind Review*: "Ongoing."

"The River Scrapes Against Night" and "The Way Back" were included in *Rough Places Plain: Poems of the Mountains*, and "Rental" appeared in *Mercy of Tides: Poems for a Beach House*, both published by Salt Marsh Pottery Press. My thanks to Margot Wizansky, who edited these anthologies.

Thanks for Monday morning writing camaraderie—words, heart, and just plain endurance—to the bpl poets. Thanks to Anne Fowler and Elizabeth Kirschner for the generosity of their friendship and their poetry critiques. Thanks to Barbara Helfgott Hyett, who reminds me that my loyalty must be to the words rather than the intention.

Thanks to Peter Conners, Nora Jones, and Thom Ward at BOA for everything they do for poetry. A particular thanks to Thom for guiding this book.

To my family, Seth and Sara, Abigail and Laura, Jacob, and my husband, Jimmy—you provide the sustaining net.

# About the Author

Wendy Mnookin is the author of three previous books, *What He Took* and *To Get Here*, published by BOA Editions, and *Guenever Speaks*, a collection of persona poems. Her poems appear in journals such as *The Greensboro Review*, *Harvard Review*, *POOL*, *Prairie Schooner*, and *Rhino*. She has won a book award from the New England Poetry Club and a Poetry Fellowship from the National Endowment for the Arts. Mnookin graduated from Radcliffe College and the Vermont College MFA Program. For many years she taught poetry in the Boston area. Her poetry website is www.wendymnookin.com.

Mnookin and her husband live in Newton, Massachusetts, where they raised their three children. Besides reading and writing, she loves walking, gardening, cooking, eating, and napping, not necessarily in that order.

# BOA Editions, Ltd.
# American Poets Continuum Series

No. 1    *The Fuhrer Bunker: A Cycle of Poems in Progress*
W. D. Snodgrass

No. 2    *She*
M. L. Rosenthal

No. 3    *Living With Distance*
Ralph J. Mills, Jr.

No. 4    *Not Just Any Death*
Michael Waters

No. 5    *That Was Then: New and Selected Poems*
Isabella Gardner

No. 6    *Things That Happen Where There Aren't Any People*
William Stafford

No. 7    *The Bridge of Change: Poems 1974–1980*
John Logan

No. 8    *Signatures*
Joseph Stroud

No. 9    *People Live Here: Selected Poems 1949–1983*
Louis Simpson

No. 10    *Yin*
Carolyn Kizer

No. 11    *Duhamel: Ideas of Order in Little Canada*
Bill Tremblay

No. 12    *Seeing It Was So*
Anthony Piccione

No. 13    *Hyam Plutzik: The Collected Poems*

No. 14    *Good Woman: Poems and a Memoir 1969–1980*
Lucille Clifton

No. 15    *Next: New Poems*
Lucille Clifton

No. 16    *Roxa: Voices of the Culver Family*
William B. Patrick

No. 17    *John Logan: The Collected Poems*

No. 18    *Isabella Gardner: The Collected Poems*

No. 19    *The Sunken Lightship*
Peter Makuck

No. 20    *The City in Which I Love You*
Li-Young Lee

No. 21    *Quilting: Poems 1987–1990*
Lucille Clifton

No. 22    *John Logan: The Collected Fiction*

No. 23    *Shenandoah and Other Verse Plays*
Delmore Schwartz

No. 24    *Nobody Lives on Arthur Godfrey Boulevard*
Gerald Costanzo

No. 25    *The Book of Names: New and Selected Poems*
Barton Sutter

No. 26    *Each in His Season*
W. D. Snodgrass

No. 27    *Wordworks: Poems Selected and New*
Richard Kostelanetz

No. 28    *What We Carry*
Dorianne Laux

No. 29    *Red Suitcase*
Naomi Shihab Nye

No. 30    *Song*
Brigit Pegeen Kelly

No. 31    *The Fuehrer Bunker: The Complete Cycle*
W. D. Snodgrass

No. 32    *For the Kingdom*
Anthony Piccione

No. 33    *The Quicken Tree*
Bill Knott

No. 34    *These Upraised Hands*
William B. Patrick

No. 35    *Crazy Horse in Stillness*
William Heyen

No. 36    *Quick, Now, Always*
Mark Irwin

No. 37    *I Have Tasted the Apple*
Mary Crow

# Colophon

*The Moon Makes Its Own Plea*, poems by Wendy Mnookin, is set in Mrs. Eaves, a typeface designed in 1996 by Zuzana Licko (1961– ) and named after Sarah Eaves. Originally John Baskerville's live-in housekeeper, she became his mistress and eventually married him after her estranged husband, Richard Eaves, died. She worked alongside Baskerville in his printing business in Birmingham, England, and completed the volumes remaining after his death in 1775.

The publication of this book is made possible, in part, by the special support of the following individuals:

Anonymous (2) ✿ Alan & Nancy Cameros

Gwen & Gary Conners ✿ Peter & Sue Durant

Rev. Anne Fowler ✿ Pete & Bev French

Jacquie & Andy Germanow, in honor of Tara

Judy & Dane Gordon ✿ Kip & Debby Hale

Tom & Illona Hansen ✿ Peter & Robin Hursh

Willy & Bob Hursh ✿ X. J. & Dorothy Kennedy

Rena Koopman ✿ Archie & Pat Kutz

Jason D. Labbe ✿ Katherine Lederer

Rosemary & Lewis Lloyd ✿ Carla E. Lynton

Marjorie Miller, in honor of Wendy Mnookin

Susan Miller & Hal Poster

Bob & Dale Mnookin, in honor of Wendy Mnookin

Boo Poulin ✿ Steven O. Russell & Phyllis Rifkin-Russell

Chris & Sarah Schoettle ✿ Vicki & Richard Schwartz

Betsy & Martin Solomon ✿ Alec Stais & Elissa Burke

Sue Stewart, in honor of Steven L. Raymond

The Wallack Family ✿ Thomas R. Ward

Patricia D. Ward-Baker ✿ F. Helmut & Caroline Weymar

Pat & Mike Wilder ✿ Glenn & Helen William

Owen & Linda Youngman

✿